Fact Finders®

ENGINEERING WONDERS

THE GOLDEN GATE BRIDGE

BY REBECCA STANBOROUGH

raintree

a Capstone company — publishers for children

Raintree is an imprint of Capstone Global Library Limited, a company incorporated in England and Wales having its registered office at 264 Banbury Road, Oxford, OX2 7DY – Registered company number: 6695582

www.raintree.co.uk
myorders@raintree.co.uk

Edited by Gena Chester, Elizabeth Johnson
Designed by Veronica Scott
Picture research by Svetlana Zhurkin
Production by Lori Blackwell
Originated by Capstone Global Library Limited
Printed and bound in China.

ISBN 978 1 4747 1178 4
20 19 18 17 16
10 9 8 7 6 5 4 3 2 1

British Library Cataloguing in Publication Data
A full catalogue record for this book is available from the British Library.

Awknowledgements
We would like to thank the following for permission to reproduce photographs: Alamy: Sueddeutsche Zeitung Photo, 25; California Historical Society, CHS2011.734, 10; Corbis, 8, San Francisco Chronicle, 24; Dreamstime: Gavin Duncan, 11 (middle); Getty Images: Underwood Archives, cover, 13 (top), 19, 20, 22; iStockphoto: narvikk, 27; Library of Congress, 6, 7, 9, 14, 16; NASA, 4; National Parks Service: Fort Point-Golden Gate, 18; Newscom: UIG/Underwood Archives, 23; Shutterstock: Creative Stall, 13 (bottom), Dr_Flash, 21 (bottom left), Jozsef Bagota, 21 (bottom middle and right), leungchopan, 11 (bottom), Luciano Mortula, 5, pmphoto, 28 (top), Robert Cicchetti, 11 (top), Stas Moroz, 28 – 29, Steve Buckley, 26, topseller, 21 (middle right); SuperStock: Underwood Photo Archives, 15. Design elements: Shutterstock.

CONTENTS

CHAPTER 1

FLOODS OF WATER, FLOODS OF PEOPLE

The Golden Gate Bridge in San Francisco, USA, is known for its beauty. Its bright orange colour stands out against the blue bay and sky. Its sweeping cables and airy towers echo the rise and fall of the mountains. But this beautiful bridge is also strong. It weighs nearly 796,000 tonnes and carries the weight of more than 112,000 cars and lorries every day. Best of all, the Golden Gate Bridge moves. To respond to fierce winds and earthquakes, this bridge was built to bounce. But how did this steel and concrete wonder come to be?

The San Francisco Bay photographed from the *Columbia* Space Shuttle.

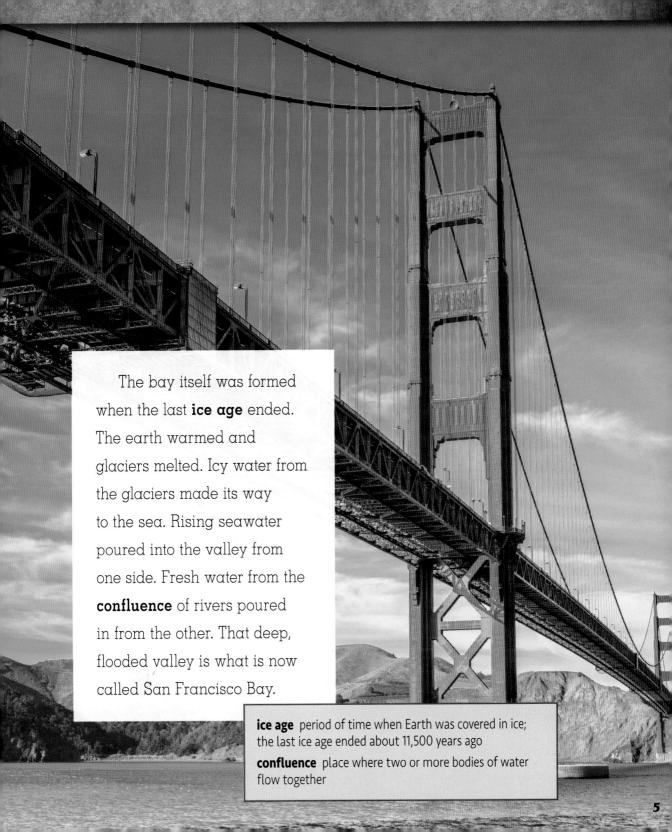

The bay itself was formed when the last **ice age** ended. The earth warmed and glaciers melted. Icy water from the glaciers made its way to the sea. Rising seawater poured into the valley from one side. Fresh water from the **confluence** of rivers poured in from the other. That deep, flooded valley is what is now called San Francisco Bay.

ice age period of time when Earth was covered in ice; the last ice age ended about 11,500 years ago

confluence place where two or more bodies of water flow together

SETTLERS ALONG THE SHORE

The waters of the bay were home to fish and shellfish. The climate was mild and the woods were full of elk and other animals. The Native American Ohlone, Coast Miwok and Patwin people enjoyed the natural resources for many generations.

Then, in 1775, Spanish explorer Juan Manuel de Ayala sailed the *San Carlos* into the bay. Within 150 years of the arrival of the Spanish, the Ohlone, Coast Miwok and Patwin people were almost gone. Then someone made a discovery that would bring a different kind of flood to the Bay Area – a cascade of new settlers. That discovery was gold.

WHY IS IT CALLED THE "GOLDEN GATE"?

In 1846, just before the **gold rush**, explorer John C. Frémont mapped the entrance to San Francisco Bay. He called the narrow opening *Chrysopylae*, meaning "Golden Gate". He believed that the bay would become a thriving harbour one day, through which wealth and trade would pour into the nation.

Gold rush!
In 1848, James Marshall found gold nuggets in water leading to California's American River. When news got out, people poured in from all over the world. In 1848, fewer than 1,000 people lived in San Francisco. Two years later, 20 times that many had arrived. By 1920, the population was over half a million people.

gold rush sudden arrival of crowds of people in search of gold

A NEW WAY TO TRAVEL

All those new Californians needed to get from one place to another. Over time, dusty trails became roads. As more and more people settled in the Bay Area, traffic increased. People needed to get from the city of San Francisco to the houses and businesses in Marin County. The only way to cross the bay was by **ferry**. People drove their cars onto a ferry. The ferry crossed the Golden Gate. Then the cars drove off the ferry and into Marin County. At peak times, the wait for a ferry could be three hours long.

Passengers ride a ferry across the bay.

ferry boat or ship that regularly carries people across a stretch of water

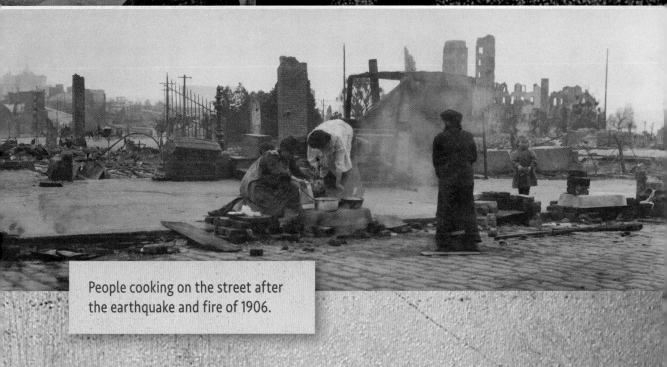

People cooking on the street after the earthquake and fire of 1906.

EARTHQUAKE!

On 18 April 1906, disaster struck. A massive earthquake hit San Francisco. Many of the houses, offices, schools, churches and hospitals collapsed. Two-thirds of the city's people were left homeless. San Franciscans had to rebuild. Many of them wanted to include a bridge over the bay in the rebuilding plans.

CHAPTER 2

A DESIGN THAT WORKS

AN UNPOPULAR FIRST DESIGN

In 1919, city officials asked San Francisco's chief **engineer**, Michael O'Shaughnessy, to find out whether a bridge could be built across the Golden Gate **Strait**. A Chicago engineer and bridge builder called Joseph Strauss believed the answer was "yes". Strauss proposed a bridge that would use two different types of support – cantilevers and suspension cables. City officials considered his design. Strauss also talked to the people of San Francisco. Many of them wanted a bridge, but some thought his design was ugly. "It looks like an upside-down rat trap," one critic said.

engineer person who uses science and mathematics to design, build or maintain machines, buildings or public works

strait narrow channel of water that connects two larger bodies of water

bedrock layer of solid rock beneath the layers of soil and loose gravel broken up by weathering

TYPES OF BRIDGE

A **CANTILEVER BRIDGE** has a central beam and supporting pillars. Metal trusses help distribute the weight of the vehicles crossing the deck of the bridge. The Ed Koch Queensboro Bridge in New York, USA is a double-decker cantilever bridge.

A **BASULE BRIDGE**, sometimes called a drawbridge, is a movable bridge with a single or double "leaf" that lifts to allow boat traffic to pass underneath. The Johnson Street Bridge, spanning the harbour in Victoria, British Columbia, was designed by Joseph Strauss.

A **SUSPENSION BRIDGE** uses vertical cables to hold up the roadway. Long supporting cables are draped over towers and anchored to concrete or to **bedrock** on either end of the bridge. Today, the longest suspension bridge in the world is the Akashi-Kaikyo Bridge in Japan. Its total suspension is 3.9 kilometres (2.42 miles).

GENIUS!

The Golden Gate Bridge was the work of many minds.

- Joseph Strauss was the bridge's champion. He surrounded himself with talented advisers.

- Leon Mouisseiff was a bridge designer from Latvia. He knew how to design strong, elegant towers made of flexible steel.

- Othmar Ammann was a Swiss engineer. He designed six of New York's most remarkable bridges.

- Charles Derleth, Jr was an expert on building in the Bay Area.

- Andrew Lawson was a **geologist**. He knew more than almost anyone else about the bedrock and earthquakes of the region.

- John Eberson and Irving Morrow were both architects. They made the Golden Gate Bridge one of the most dramatic bridges in the world.

- Charles Alton Ellis was the mathematical mind behind the bridge. Everyone wanted the bridge to be lighter and more graceful than other suspension bridges. But the bridge also had to be longer and stronger than the others. Ellis had to use maths to test the strength and flexibility of the bridge. For 20 months, he calculated and recalculated.

geologist someone who studies minerals, rocks and soil

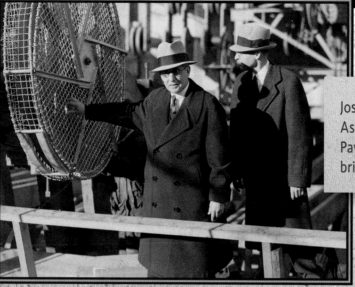

Joseph Strauss (left) and the Assistant Chief Engineer William Payne discuss the details of the bridge design.

THE FORCES THAT STRESS A BRIDGE

Bridges have to be able to bear two types of load: dead loads and live loads. Firstly, every bridge has to be strong enough to bear the weight of its own materials. That weight is called the "dead" load. Secondly, every bridge has to be able to bear the weight of whatever is crossing the bridge. That weight is called the "live" load. Live loads also include water droplets and wind forces. Loads either push the parts of the bridge together (compression) or pull them apart (tension). The Golden Gate Bridge handles these forces in two ways: the towers bear the compression forces, and the cables bear the tension forces.

CHAPTER 3

CONSTRUCTION BEGINS

THE WORK FORCE

It was difficult to design the bridge. But it was even more difficult to build it. Fortunately, there was no shortage of able workers. When construction began in 1933, the country was deep in the **Depression**. Jobs were hard to find. People came from far away to compete for jobs on the bridge crew. Pay was very good because the workers faced danger every day.

PAID FOR
TO THIS PORT
Every Dollar
20 More Meals

Depression (also known as the Great Depression) deepest and longest-lasting economic downturn in the history of the Western industrialized world

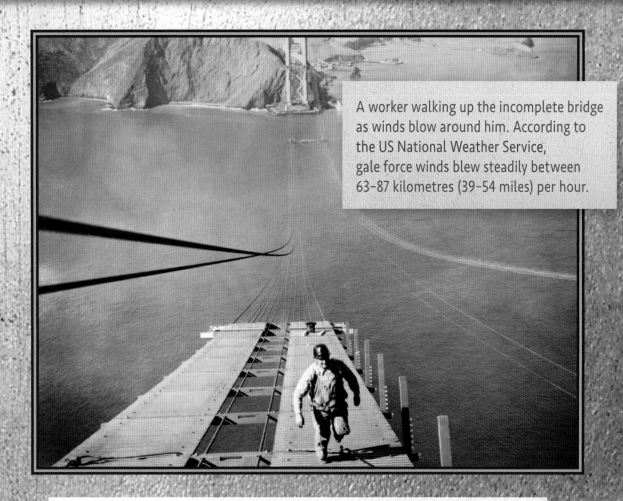

A worker walking up the incomplete bridge as winds blow around him. According to the US National Weather Service, gale force winds blew steadily between 63–87 kilometres (39–54 miles) per hour.

Gale force winds bullied them as they hammered and welded 152 metres (500 feet) off the ground. When fog rolled in, they could barely see. Water droplets made every step slick. And it was very cold up on the catwalks. Some workers even got lead poisoning from the **primer** paint used on the steel. Once, a small earthquake struck during the workday. Everyone grabbed the beams to avoid being thrown off the bridge.

primer base coat of paint that goes on before the main colour

Even with all of these dangers, people needed the work. Men lined up every day – waiting for someone to be injured so that they could step in. Most workers had to belong to a **union** to get one of the jobs on the bridge. While unions helped members who worked to get decent pay, only a select few received membership. Unions of that era were not open to minorities. Very few women or people from ethnic minorities worked on the bridge.

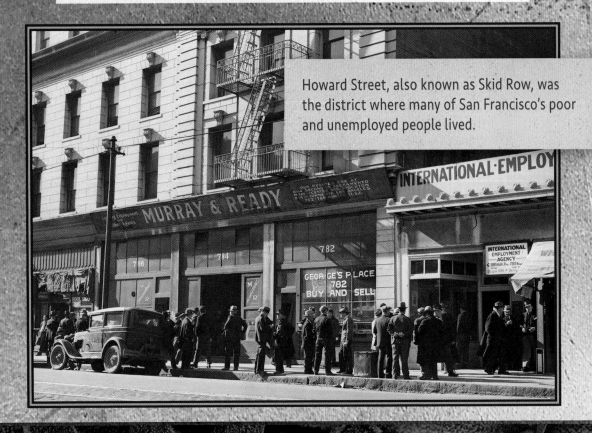

Howard Street, also known as Skid Row, was the district where many of San Francisco's poor and unemployed people lived.

ANCHORING THE BRIDGE

The first step was to test the strength of the bedrock at the bottom of the bay. They needed to be sure the towers would stay in place. Geologists drilled holes in the bedrock. They looked at the **density** of the stone. They found that it was solid enough to hold up the towers.

Then work could begin on the two concrete **anchorages**. On the north end of the bridge, workers drove steel into the bedrock to make a frame. Then they poured 139,150 cubic metres (182,000 cubic yards) of concrete into the frame. The hard concrete would form the base to hold the towers.

The south anchorage was harder to build. It had to be located 340 metres (1,125 feet) off shore, in the churning bay. Divers worked in the freezing water. They dove 30 metres (100 feet) below the surface. They blasted holes in the bedrock using explosives. They worked in 20-minute shifts in the dark. They worked against the fierce pull of the tides.

union group of workers who try to gain more rights, such as fair pay and safer jobs, for workers

density amount of mass an object or substance has, based on a unit of volume

anchorage something that provides a secure hold; a massive masonry or concrete construction securing a cable at each end

Once the divers had blasted wells for the foundation, builders made a moat-like structure. They pumped out the seawater. Workers now had a dry area in which to build the rest of the anchorage. With the seawater gone, they could attach the steel foundation to bedrock. Then they poured in 99,390 cubic metres (130,000 cubic yards) of concrete. Together, the north and south anchorages support the towers and the cables that hold up the whole bridge.

Two workers sitting on top of the main tower, 227 metres (746 feet) above the water.

BUILDING THE TOWERS

Each of the two towers rises 227 metres (746 feet) above the waterline. They appear to be made of solid steel. But the towers are made of hollow, beehive-like cells. Each cell is a 1 metre (3½ foot) square. The towers can sway in all four directions in response to wind, temperature changes and earthquakes.

To build the towers, workers stood on **scaffolds**. They had to be raised each time a new level was built. A total of 404 cells were connected with more than 600,000 **rivets** in each tower. Two steel "saddles" sit atop each tower to hold the cables. Altogether, the towers contain around 39,900 tonnes of steel.

Did you know?

Inside the towers, there are 37 kilometres (23 miles) of ladders and a lift running top to bottom.

scaffold temporary framework or platforms used to support workers and materials
rivet short steel bolt that fastens two pieces of metal together

INTERNATIONAL ORANGE

Everyone had an opinion about what colour the bridge should be painted. Some people wanted classic grey. Others worried that ships would not see a grey bridge in the fog. The US Navy wanted yellow and black stripes so the bridge would be highly visible. The US Army Air Corps rallied for red and white stripes. In the end, the bridge designers chose "international orange", a colour very close to the red primer paint that covered the steel during construction. International orange, they felt, would contrast with the blue sky and call attention to the natural beauty of the hills.

The towers (left; not shown to scale) were designed in the art deco style. The repeating cells of the towers become smaller as the towers rise. This "stepped-back" look is common in art deco architecture such as the Empire State and Chrysler buildings in New York City. This style appears light and graceful. The towers could be both light and strong because of advances in steelwork.

CHAPTER 4

SPANNING THE BAY

DRAPING THE CABLES

The cables are not solid ropes of steel. They are woven from more than 128,700 kilometres (80,000 miles) of steel strands. Because of their weight, the cables had to be spun together on site, in the air. The steelworkers used a sort of loom to twist the wires together in bundles. In each cable, there are 61 bundles. In each bundle, there are 452 wires. Once the cables were assembled, they were clamped with iron bands and wrapped in wire **sheaths** to protect the surface. Then they were draped over the towers and anchored in place. Each of the cables is around 1 metre (3 feet) in diameter and 2,330 metres (7,650 feet) long.

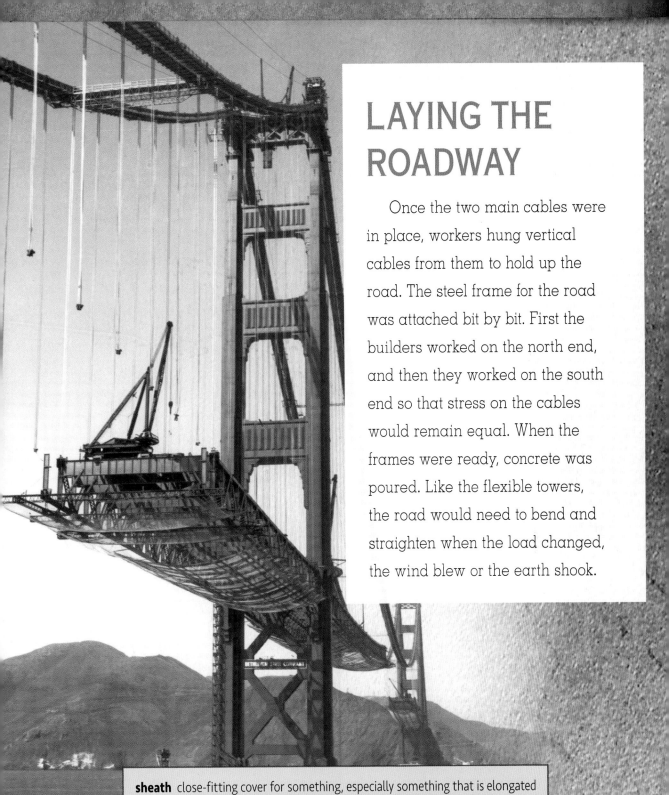

LAYING THE ROADWAY

Once the two main cables were in place, workers hung vertical cables from them to hold up the road. The steel frame for the road was attached bit by bit. First the builders worked on the north end, and then they worked on the south end so that stress on the cables would remain equal. When the frames were ready, concrete was poured. Like the flexible towers, the road would need to bend and straighten when the load changed, the wind blew or the earth shook.

sheath close-fitting cover for something, especially something that is elongated

WORKING SAFELY

Joseph Strauss and construction engineer Russell Cone wanted to make sure that workers stayed safe. For the first time on any building site in the United States, workers were required to wear hard hats. When steelworkers became ill from inhaling lead dust, they were given masks to keep the dust out of their lungs. They also wore special goggles that cut down on the glare from the sun and the sea. Most importantly, Strauss purchased a net that cost $130,000. He strung it up beneath the bridge. The net saved 19 men from being killed when they fell.

Accidents still happened. One man, Kermit Moore, was crushed by a beam. And on 17 February 1937, 10 men died when their scaffold collapsed and tore through the net. Their names are engraved on a plaque at the south end of the bridge.

The safety net (seen underneath the steel cross sections) saved each of the workers pictured here.

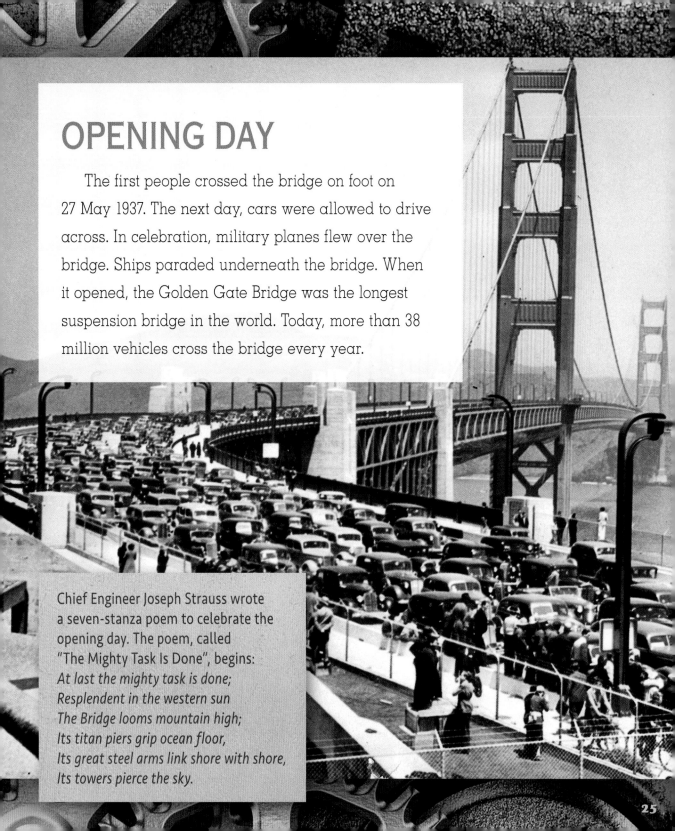

OPENING DAY

The first people crossed the bridge on foot on 27 May 1937. The next day, cars were allowed to drive across. In celebration, military planes flew over the bridge. Ships paraded underneath the bridge. When it opened, the Golden Gate Bridge was the longest suspension bridge in the world. Today, more than 38 million vehicles cross the bridge every year.

Chief Engineer Joseph Strauss wrote a seven-stanza poem to celebrate the opening day. The poem, called "The Mighty Task Is Done", begins:
At last the mighty task is done;
Resplendent in the western sun
The Bridge looms mountain high;
Its titan piers grip ocean floor,
Its great steel arms link shore with shore,
Its towers pierce the sky.

CHAPTER 5

ACROSS THE BAY, ACROSS THE YEARS

CHANGING WITH THE TIMES

In 1951, high winds forced the bridge to close. After the storm passed, inspectors checked the bridge. They decided to add more **bracing** to make the bridge safer. Twice more, in 1982 and 1983, the bridge had to be closed when storms brought winds of more than 113 kilometres (70 miles) per hour. The bridge was undamaged, thanks to the earlier bracing.

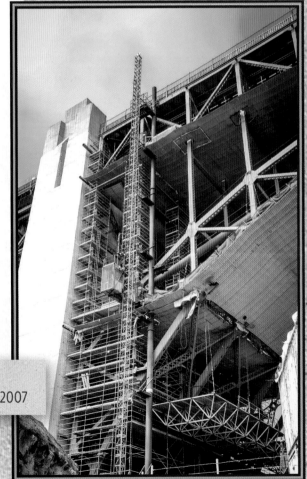

repairs being carried out in 2007

In 1989, the Loma Prieta earthquake ripped through San Francisco. It caused 68 deaths and extensive damage to buildings. The earthquake started 97 kilometres (60 miles) away, so the bridge was not damaged. Engineers decided to **retrofit** the bridge anyway, in case a major earthquake struck closer next time.

bracing ties and rods used for supporting and strengthening various parts of a structure
retrofit provide something with new parts that were not available when it was originally built

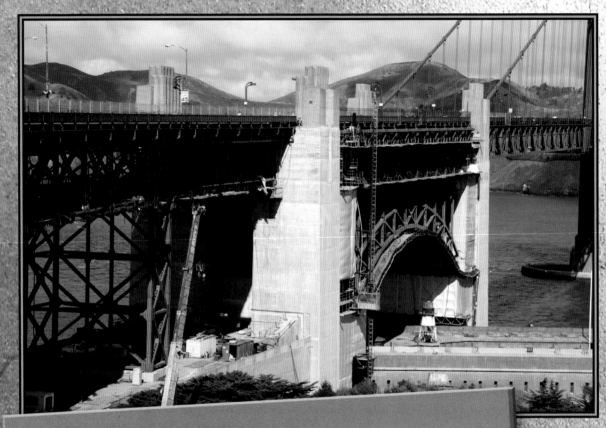

Did you know?

In 1977, the bridge was 40 years old. The roadway was cracking. The cracks were filled with salt used to de-ice the road. Engineers worried that the salt would eat into the steel, so the roadway was replaced. The new road was stronger – and thousands of tonnes lighter.

The Golden Gate Bridge means a lot to San Francisco and the United States. Engineers continue to make changes to keep it in safe working order. Salt, fog, wind, earthquakes and other forces can damage the bridge. It is constantly being examined, repaired and repainted.

Anchored deep in the earth, soaring into the sky, the Golden Gate Bridge is a wonder of engineering. It took a talented team of engineers to design a bridge that could bear such massive loads so gracefully. And it took many other people to make those designs a reality. The parts of the bridge itself – trusses, cables, towers and anchorages – pull together to create safe passage for thousands of people crossing San Francisco Bay every day.

GLOSSARY

anchorage something that provides a secure hold; a massive masonry or concrete construction securing a cable at each end

bedrock layer of solid rock beneath the layers of soil and loose gravel broken up by weathering

bracing ties and rods used for supporting and strengthening various parts of a structure

confluence place where two or more bodies of water flow together

density amount of mass an object or substance has, based on a unit of volume

Depression (also known as the Great Depression) deepest and longest-lasting economic downturn in the history of the Western industrialized world

engineer person who uses science and mathematics to design, build or maintain machines, buildings or public works

ferry boat or ship that regularly carries people across a stretch of water

geologist someone who studies minerals, rocks and soil; geology is the study of how Earth was formed and how it changes

gold rush sudden arrival of crowds of people in search of gold

ice age period of time when Earth was covered in ice; the last ice age ended about 11,500 years ago

primer base coat of paint that goes on before the main colour

retrofit provide something with new parts that were not available when it was originally built

rivet strong metal bolt that is used to fasten something together

scaffold temporary framework or platforms used to support workers and materials

sheath close-fitting cover for something, especially something that is elongated

strait narrow channel of water that connects two larger bodies of water

union group of workers who try to gain more rights, such as fair pay and safer jobs, for workers

BOOKS

Fabulous Bridges (Superstructures), Ian Graham (Franklin Watts, 2012)

Super Cool Construction Activities with Max Axiom (Max Axiom Science and Engineering Activities), Tammy Enz (Raintree, 2015)

The World's Most Amazing Bridges (Landmark Top Tens), Michael Hurley (Raintree, 2012)

WEBSITES

www.bbc.co.uk/schools/gcsebitesize/history/mwh/usa/walldepressionrev1.shtml
Learn more about the US Wall Street Crash and Great Depression.

http://goldengatebridge.org/photos/
Take a look at more photos of this amazing bridge, from construction to present day.

COMPREHENSION QUESTIONS

1. Why was the south anchorage so much harder to build than the north anchorage? Give evidence from the text to support your answer.

2. Strauss' first bridge design incorporated cantilever elements. What is a cantilever bridge?

3. The bridge tower's beehive cell structure allows it to sway in all four directions. Why is it important for the bridge to be able to do this?

INDEX